D1455898

PERFECT PETS

Small Birds

Melissa Stewart

BENCHMARK BOOKS

MARSHALL CAVENDISH

NEW YORK

Marshall Cavendish Corporation
99 White Plains Rd.
Tarrytown, NY 10591
www.marshallcavendish.com

©2003 by Marshall Cavendish

Library of Congress Cataloging-in-Publication Data

Stewart, Melissa.
        Small birds / by Melissa Stewart.
                p. cm. – (Perfect Pets)
        Includes bibliographical references (p.) and index.
Summary: Surveys the history of keeping birds as pets and outlines
the needs and habits of some common pet birds.
        ISBN 0-7614-1397-9
1. Cage birds—Juvenile literature. [1. Birds as pets. 2. Pets.]
I. Title. II. Series.

SF461.35.S74 2002
636.6'8—dc21

2001043914

Photo research by Candlepants, Inc.

Cover Photo: Animals Animals / J. & P. Wegner

The photographs in this book are used by permission and through the
courtesy of; Photo Researchers: Anthony Mercieca Photo, 1; Jacana, 7;
Jeanne White, 10; Carolyn A. McKeone, 12; Danny Brass, 27. Animals
Animals: Robert Maier, 3, 11, 14, 18; J. & P. Wegner, 6, 8, 24, 28; Gerard
Lacz, 13; Renee Stockdale, 25 (top & bottom), back cover.; Austin J.
Stevens, 26; Art Resource / The Newark Museum: 4. Photofest: 17 Hulton
/ Archive by Getty Images: 20, 21. Image Bank / Guido Alberto Rossi: 22.

Printed in Hong Kong
6 5 4 3 2 1

For Gerard and Princer

This watercolor depicts a pet bird perching on the hand of a ruler of India's Mughal Empire.

For thousands

of years, people have admired birds for their bright colors, their beautiful songs, and their ability to fly. These are some of the reasons birds are such popular pets.

No one knows how long ago people began keeping caged birds. The Sumerians, a group of people who lived in the Middle East about five thousand years ago, had a word for *birdcage* in their language. In ancient India, brightly colored pet birds were proudly displayed during festive parades. The ancient Chinese and Persians also kept small birds.

There are more than nine thousand different **species**, or kinds, of birds, but only a few make good pets. These birds are easy to tame, feed, and care for.

Small parrots, such as the parakeet, and finches, such as the canary, are the most popular pet birds. They are both colorful

Parakeets, such as these four males, make good pets. They are cheerful companions and are easy to take care of.

and cheerful. Finches sing beautifully, and parrots can learn to say words. These birds are also fairly inexpensive and small enough to keep in most homes. They eat seeds, which are easy to find and store.

In the wild, parrots and finches live in large **flocks** made up of family groups. As pets, they learn to think of their human owners as family members. Most small birds don't like to be touched by humans, but parakeets, canaries, and their close relatives can usually be trained to sit on a person's finger. Over time, they learn to trust and even show affection for their owners.

In the wild, flocks of parakeets often perch together in trees.

Today, budgies come in a wide variety of colors.

Parakeets

are small parrots that originally lived in Southeast Asia and Australia. About 2,300 years ago, a Greek ruler named Alexander the Great invaded northern India and brought the first parrots to Europe. The Alexandrine parakeet is named after this ancient warrior. Eventually, the Romans conquered the Greeks. The Romans also carried home parrots from Asia, India, and Africa, and kept the talking birds as pets.

Most of the parakeets that people keep today are descended from birds that came from Australia. They are known as **budgerigars**, or budgies for short. In one of the languages spoken by native Australians, or aborigines, *budgerigar* means "pretty bird" or "good bird."

Budgie parents snuggle with their new babies.

In the Wild

Wild budgies live in the Outback—the **semiarid** and desert area in the middle of Australia. Luckily, these birds have what it takes to survive in dry places. They can go up to a month without taking a single drink of water. What's their secret? They can get all the water they need from the seeds they eat. When water is in really short supply, budgies stop laying eggs.

When rain finally falls, budgies flock to watering holes, build nests, and lay eggs right away. Budgie parents can raise three families within a few months, and the youngsters start to have families of their own when they are only three months old. At this rate, it doesn't take long for a flock to grow. But when watering holes start to disappear, budgie populations shrink again—until another heavy rain comes.

In 1840, scientist John Gould brought the first wild budgies to Europe. A few years later, Gould's brother-in-law, Charles Coxen, began **breeding** and selling the birds. By 1880, parakeets had become common pets. Today, parakeets are the most popular caged bird in the world. More than 12 million pet parakeets live in homes across the United States. Many experts believe there may be more caged parakeets than wild ones.

A budgie perches atop a toy.

Choose your favorite color! Budgies come in many different shades.

Gould's budgies were light green on the chest and back, with lemon-yellow faces and black and brown bars on their wings and throats. Because Coxen and later breeders carefully selected males and females to mate, budgies now come in a variety of colors. Some are pure white or bright yellow, while others are cobalt blue or pinkish mauve. Most budgies are some combination of these colors.

Budgies and other parakeets are about 8 inches (20 centimeters) long and weigh nearly 2 ounces (57 grams). Besides being colorful, they are playful and learn tricks quickly. But parakeets are best known for talking. These birds do not understand what they are saying. They simply copy, or **mimic**, the sounds you make.

Some parakeets learn faster than others. Some can learn to say words they hear when family members speak to one another. A few can even mimic the sound of a ringing telephone or creaking floorboards.

Most of the time, it takes a lot of patience to teach a parakeet to speak. Begin by choosing one short word and saying it over and over again until the bird copies you. Women and children are often more successful trainers because they have higher-pitched voices. While your bird may never be really talkative, most parakeets can learn to mimic a dozen words or short phrases.

Lovebirds, like these two, are very affectionate with each other.

A Look at Lovebirds

Like parakeets, lovebirds are small, brightly colored parrots that are sometimes kept as pets. Lovebirds are a bit smaller than parakeets. They have large heads, stocky bodies, and short tails. Wild lovebirds live in Africa and on the island of Madagascar. These birds usually sit close to their mates with their heads touching. They are intelligent and playful but more difficult to train to talk than parakeets.

13

Zebra finches have brightly colored beaks and cheeks.

Finches

are very common birds. You may have seen gold finches at a backyard bird feeder. Many people keep zebra finches and Lady Gouldian finches as pets. They are easy to care for and inexpensive, and the males have a sweet song. But true bird lovers prize canaries above all other finches. Canaries are more expensive than their relatives, but many people think their colorful feathers, cheerful personality, and beautiful song make them worth the cost.

Spanish sailors brought the first canaries to Europe in the late 1400s. They discovered the birds in the Canary Islands, off the coast of Africa. Wild canaries also live on the Madeira Islands, the Azores, and the Cape Verde Islands. They are usually olive green or greenish yellow with some brown.

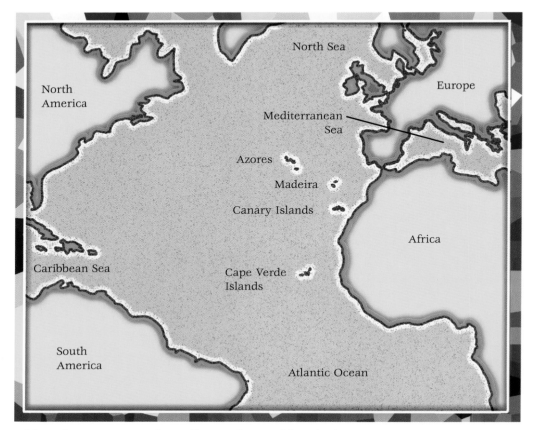

Although pet canaries live all over the world with their owners, wild canaries live only on a few islands in the Atlantic Ocean.

Canaries build nests of dry moss, feathers, and grass in tall, thick shrubs or in trees and lay four to six pale blue eggs at a time. If the weather is good and food is plentiful, they may have as many as four families a year.

Cartoon Canary

In 1942, Tweety Bird made his first appearance, in a cartoon called *A Tale of Two Kitties*. Five years later, the sweet, lovable canary was paired with archenemy Sylvester the cat, and an elderly woman named Granny was also added to the cast. In 1948, *Tweety Pie*, the first cartoon featuring all three characters, won an Oscar.

Since then, "I tawt I taw a puddy tat!" has become a phrase recognized around the world. Although the cartoon series ended in 1964, Tweety Bird lived on in comic books until 1984 and can still be seen in television reruns. In 1996, Tweety and Sylvester appeared in the popular movie *Space Jam*, and in 1998, they were featured on a U.S. postage stamp.

Tweety Bird is one of the most popular cartoon characters in America.

Some canaries are prized for their singing ability.

Because

bird breeders have carefully mated males and females, canaries now come in a variety of colors. Some canaries have special features or are especially good singers. The crested Norwich has a decorative group of feathers on top of its head. The Scotch fancy is a slender bird with high, arched shoulders. The Manchester is larger than other canaries.

Male St. Andreasburg canaries are the most melodious in the world. These birds, which are raised by breeders living in the Harz Mountains of Germany, belong to a group of canaries known as **rollers**. Their soft, mellow song is a complex set of rolling trills. They sing with their beaks almost closed. Other male canaries, called **choppers**, sing with their heads thrown back and their beaks wide open. Their melodies have a wilder and freer sound. Female canaries cannot sing as well as males, but they chirp cheerfully and deliver simple trills.

In the late 1600s, a French canary trainer named Hervieux de Chanteloup and his canaries performed elaborate concerts. As many as one hundred canaries sang while others danced. Recently, a Russian canary trainer named Fyodor Fokenko bred canaries that could sing bass. As a result, he was able to create the first canary choir that performed the full range of musical parts: soprano, alto, tenor, and bass. His choir could perform more than eighty classical pieces, including "Moonlight" sonata by German composer Ludwig van Beethoven and a variety of waltzes written by Austrian composer Johann Strauss.

These trainers dedicated their entire lives to their canaries, but you can teach a canary to sing a few simple songs much more easily. Begin by playing a recording of a well-trained canary. If your bird seems to have trouble imitating the tune, turn out the lights. The dark room may help it. Singing, whistling, or playing the piano may also encourage your canary to sing.

Dr. Nicholas Pastore was another famous canary trainer. He conditioned his canaries to "ask" for their food.

A Welsh miner with his canary. Canaries are still used as a safety measure against poisonous gas in mines.

Canaries Save Lives

Long ago, coal miners in Great Britain realized that canaries are fifteen times more sensitive than people to **carbon monoxide**, a poisonous gas that may build up in underground tunnels. From that point on, miners in Great Britain and the rest of Europe brought canaries to work with them. Someone always kept an eye on the little yellow birds. If they passed out, the miners knew they were in danger. They hurried out of the mine and revived the canaries in tiny oxygen tents.

In 1983, the National Coal Board in the United Kingdom tried to phase out the use of canaries in coal mines. By that time, scientists had developed devices that could accurately detect carbon monoxide. But many miners refused to stop using canaries. They trusted their little feathered friends more than high-tech scientific instruments. The board eventually agreed to let the miners keep using canaries.

Your small bird's cage should be a safe and roomy environment.

All small birds

should be kept in cages—the larger the better. Plastic cages are the best choice for canaries and other finches. They are lightweight and easy to clean. Parakeets will chew on plastic, so they need to live in metal cages. Think carefully about where you keep your bird's cage. It should be in a quiet corner of a room that people use often. Make sure it is not too close to heat or air vents and does not receive direct sunlight.

The cage should have several perches spaced far enough apart for the bird to stretch its wings. Line the bottom with plain paper to catch falling feathers, seed hulls, and droppings. Do not use newspaper. The ink can make your bird sick. You may want to add a few toys to the cage. Parakeets like to climb ladders and ring bells. Canaries prefer swings.

A budgie enjoying its millet!

You will also need separate food and water dishes in the cage. Ask a pet store worker to recommend the right kind for your bird. Also ask how you should bathe your bird.

A pet store is the best place to buy seeds for birds. Each kind of bird prefers a specific blend of seeds. Small birds may also eat greens or grated carrots once in a while, and should be given a small amount of grit or gravel. These materials help a bird break down food in its **gizzard**. You may also want to hang some **millet** in its cage, and occasionally add wheat germ oil to your bird's food. A **cuttlefish bone** will help your pet keep its beak sharp and get the minerals it needs.

Small birds love to play with toys. Here, two lovebirds try a seesaw.

When your pet bird has learned to trust you, it will perch on your finger.

Most caged birds are happiest when they have some time to fly free each day. But first you need to train your pet to trust you and come back to its cage when it feels tired. Begin by opening the cage and holding your finger close to a perch until the bird hops on. After your pet has done this several times, slowly move your finger out of the cage, and your bird will flutter off. If it will not return to the cage, gently drop a cloth over your bird and carry it carefully back to its cage. Eventually, your bird will learn that your finger is a safe place.

Small birds need a lot of attention. Make sure you spend time with your bird every day.

Before you let your bird out of its cage, always make sure that no small children or other pets are in the room. Houseplants might make your bird sick, so move them to another room. Close all doors and windows. Until your bird is used to the room, pull blinds over the windows and cover the mirrors with sheets so your pet won't fly into them.

Most important, your pet bird needs attention every day. If a small bird is left alone for long periods, it will get sick. You may leave the bird alone for a short time if you turn on a radio to keep it company. But if no one is home for most of the day, you should buy two birds. Then they can keep each other company. However, if you have two birds, they will be less likely to talk, sing, or play with you.

Having a pet bird can be a lot of fun, but like other pets, birds need special care and attention.

This bright-eyed canary would make a great pet.

How to Choose a Small Bird

Look at a bird carefully before buying it. It should have sleek, neat feathers and clear, bright eyes. The bird should also be active and alert. Male parakeets, which have a small spot of blue above their back, learn to talk more quickly and are often more affectionate. Do not buy a canary between July and October. This is when the birds **molt**, or lose their feathers. Any change in the canary's environment will upset it. November or December is the best time to buy a canary, but be sure to keep it warm on the way home.

Fun Facts

According to *The Guinness Book of Records*, a parakeet named Sparkie learned 531 words, 383 sentences, and eight complete nursery rhymes over an eight year period. Sparkie became famous when he appeared in television commercials for birdseed and made a recording that explained how a person should teach a bird to talk.

Birds spend almost all their time looking for and eating food. You can tell what a bird eats by looking at the shape of its beak. The beaks of parrots and finches are short and tough. They are perfect for cracking open seeds.

A caged bird sleeps standing up. In this position, the weight of its body pushes down and the muscles and tendons in its legs flex, causing its toes to form a clamp around the perch.

A bird's feathers are made of the same material as your hair and fingernails. The feathers grow out of little tubes in a bird's skin.

Glossary

breeding: carefully choosing male and female birds to mate so that chicks will look and behave in certain ways

budgerigars: a kind of parakeet that came from Australia and is a very popular pet bird

carbon monoxide: a very toxic gas that is colorless and odorless

chopper: a male canary with a simple, wild, and free song

cuttlefish bone: a hard body part that comes from an animal closely related to octopuses and squids

flock: a group of birds that feed and travel together

gizzard: the part of a bird's digestive system that breaks down hard foods, such as seeds and nuts

millet: a plant related to wheat that can provide a pet bird with important nutrients

mimic: to imitate or copy

molt: to shed feathers

roller: a male canary with a soft, mellow song consisting of a complex set of rolling trills

semiarid: description of an area that gets very little rainfall each year

species: a category of animals that share certain characteristics

Find Out More About Small Birds

Books

Evans, Mark. *ASPCA Pet Care Guides for Kids: Birds* New York:
Dorling Kindersley, 1993.

Gutman, Bill. *Becoming Your Bird's Best Friend* Brookfield, CT:
Millbrook, 1996.

Johnston, Madeline E. *A Perfect Pet.* Santa Fe, NM:
Azro Press, 2000

Lofting, Hugh. *Doctor Dolittle and the Green Canary* Philadelphia:
Lippincott, 1950.

Piers, Helen. *Taking Care of Your Parakeet (A Young Pet Owner's Guide).*
Hauppague, NY: Barrons, 1993.

Walker, Pam. *My Parakeet.* Danbury, CT: Children's Press, 2001.

Websites

International Canary and Finch Society

http://www3.upatsix.com/ics

Check out this site to learn more about this organization. They may
sponsor meetings or events in your area.

The World's Smartest Budgie

http://talkingbudgie.homestead.com

Learn all about Betty, a parakeet that knows more than two hundred
words and can string words together into phrases and sentences. Can
she truly understand human speech?

Index

Page numbers in boldface are illustrations.

About the Author

Melissa Stewart has always loved animals and nature. She earned a bachelor's degree in biology from Union College and a master's degree in science and environmental journalism from New York University. She has written more than two dozen nonfiction books for children and a variety of magazine articles for adults and children. Her work has appeared in *Natural New England*, *Science World*, *Wild Outdoor World*, and *American Heritage of Invention & Technology*. Ms. Stewart lives in Marlborough, Massachusetts. While she was growing up, her family had four dogs, three cats, two pigs, and a pet budgie named Bert.